P r e f a c e

Firearm safety is the law in California. Every firearm owner should understand and follow firearm safety practices, have a basic familiarity with the operation and handling of their firearm, and be fully aware of the responsibility of firearm ownership. Pursuant to Penal Code section 26840, any person who acquires a firearm must have a Firearm Safety Certificate (FSC), unless they are statutorily exempt from the FSC requirement. To obtain an FSC, a person must pass a Department of Justice (DOJ) written test on firearm safety. The test is administered by DOJ Certified Instructors, who are often located at firearms dealerships.

This study guide provides the basic firearm safety information necessary to pass the test. Following the firearm safety information in this guide will help reduce the potential for accidental deaths and injuries, particularly those involving children, caused by the unsafe handling and storing of firearms.

In addition to safety information, this study guide provides a general summary of the state laws that govern the sale and use of firearms. Finally, there is a glossary that defines the more technical terms used in the study guide.

Simply reading this study guide will not make you a safe firearm owner. To be a safe firearm owner you must practice the firearm safety procedures described in the following pages.

Table of Contents

Chapter 4: Firearm Ownership

Prohibited Firearms Transfers and Straw Purchases 34

Chapter 5: Firearms Laws

Introduction

WHY FIREARM SAFETY?

Firearm safety is important to all Californians. No one wants firearm accidents to happen yet they do everyday. Firearm accidents involving children are especially disturbing. Studies show that easy access to loaded firearms in homes is often a contributing factor in accidental shootings of children.

While there may be no way to guarantee safety, firearm owners can take steps to help prevent many accidental shootings. This study guide will give you valuable information to help you become a safe and responsible firearm owner.

FIREARM SAFETY IS THE LAW

The intent of the California Legislature in enacting the FSC law is to ensure that persons who obtain firearms have a basic familiarity with those firearms, including but not limited to, the safe handling and storage of those firearms. It is not the intent of the Legislature to require an FSC for the mere possession of a firearm. (Pen. Code, § 31610.)

FIREARM SAFETY CERTIFICATE INFORMATION

To obtain an FSC, you must take the DOJ written test and receive a passing score of at least 75% (the information needed to pass the test is contained in this study guide).

An FSC is valid for five years from the date of issuance. If your FSC is lost, stolen or destroyed, a replacement may be obtained from the DOJ Certified Instructor who issued your original FSC.

Pursuant to Penal Code section 31700, there are exemptions from the FSC requirement including, but not limited to:

- Federal Firearms License Collectors with a Certificate of Eligibility (for Curio and Relic transactions only);

- Active, active reserve, or honorably retired military;

- Carry Concealed Weapon (CCW) permit holders; and

- Persons who have completed Peace Officers Standards and Training (POST) (Pen. Code, § 832) firearms training.

For a complete list of exemptions visit the DOJ website at http://oag.ca.gov/firearms or contact the DOJ Bureau of Firearms, General Information Line at (916) 227-7527. You are required to provide documentation of your exemption to the firearms dealer each time you acquire a firearm.

CAUSES OF FIREARM ACCIDENTS

Ignorance and carelessness are major causes of firearm accidents. To help reduce the number of firearm accidents, it is critical that gun safety rules are understood and practiced at all times by every family member.

Following are some examples of firearm accidents that could have been avoided if the basic gun safety rules had been practiced:

> *Two young children playing in their home found a loaded handgun with the magazine removed on a bedside table. One child was injured when the handgun was fired.*

> *A handgun owner assumed a firearm was unloaded. While cleaning it, he accidentally fired the handgun, causing injury to himself.*

> *A hunter was walking with his finger loosely on the trigger of his rifle. Distracted by a sudden noise behind him, he turned and accidentally fired, injuring his buddy walking nearby.*

Knowing the safety rules and applying them most of the time is not enough. Firearm accidents can happen even to a person who knows the safety rules, but is careless in following them. For example, you may think you can leave your loaded firearm out on the kitchen table just for a moment while you go outside to turn off the garden hose. Although you know you should never leave a firearm where a child may find it, you carelessly think it will be alright "just this once."

REMEMBER: Ignorance and carelessness can result in firearm accidents. Basic gun safety rules must be applied ALL OF THE TIME.

PREVENTING MISUSE TRAGEDIES

It's a fact that many depressed, intoxicated, substance abusive, or enraged individuals commit suicide every year with firearms, usually handguns. The developmental issues associated with adolescence make teenagers particularly susceptible to this unfortunate outcome. Safe and responsible firearm storage, particularly when a member of the household is experiencing one of the aforementioned conditions, can help prevent tragedies.

BECOMING A SAFE AND RESPONSIBLE FIREARM OWNER

Becoming a safe firearm owner is similar to becoming a safe driver—you combine a good working knowledge of the equipment, the basic skills of operation, and a mind set dedicated to safe and responsible usage and storage.

This means you must have:

- Respect for the danger of firearms;
- An awareness and concern about the possible safety hazards related to firearms; and
- A desire to learn and practice safe conduct with firearms.

Developing a mind set for safe and responsible firearm usage and storage is the first step in actually becoming a responsible firearm owner. The next step is building your knowledge of firearms and gun safety, which you can do by reading and understanding the information in this study guide. The final steps are becoming skillful in handling firearms and using the safety knowledge that you have acquired.

CHAPTER 1
Gun Safety Rules

This chapter will introduce you to specific gun safety rules to give you a better understanding of firearm safety.

THE SIX BASIC GUN SAFETY RULES

There are six basic gun safety rules for gun owners to understand and practice at all times:

1. Treat all guns as if they are loaded.

2. Keep the gun pointed in the safest possible direction.

3. Keep your finger off the trigger until you are ready to shoot.

4. Know your target, its surroundings, and beyond.

5. Know how to properly operate your gun.

6. Store your gun safely and securely to prevent unauthorized use. Guns and ammunition should be stored separately.

1. Treat all guns as if they are loaded.

- Always assume that a gun is loaded even if you think it is unloaded.

- Every time a gun is handled for any reason, check to see that it is unloaded. For specific instructions on how to unload a firearm, see Chapter 3.

- If you are unable to check a gun to see if it is unloaded, leave it alone and seek help from someone more knowledgeable about guns.

2. Keep the gun pointed in the safest possible direction.

- Always be aware of where the gun is pointing. A "safe direction" is one
- where an accidental discharge of the gun will not cause injury or damage.

- Only point a gun at an object that you intend to shoot.

- Never point a gun toward yourself or another person.

3. Keep your finger off the trigger until you are ready to shoot.

- Always keep your finger off the trigger and outside the trigger guard until you are ready to shoot.

- Even though it may be comfortable to rest your finger on the trigger, it is unsafe.

- If you are moving around with your finger on the trigger and stumble or fall, you could inadvertently pull the trigger.

- Sudden loud noises or movements can result in an accidental discharge because there is a natural tendency to tighten the muscles when startled.

- The trigger is for firing, the handle is for handling.

4. Know your target, its surroundings, and beyond.

- Check that the areas in front of and behind your target are safe before shooting.

- Be aware that if the bullet misses or completely passes through the target, it could strike a person or object.

- Identify the target and make sure it is what you intend to shoot. If you are in doubt, DON'T SHOOT!

- Never fire at a target that is only a movement, color, sound or unidentifiable shape.

- Be aware of all the people around you before you shoot.

5. Know how to properly operate your gun.

- It is important to become thoroughly familiar with your gun. You should know its mechanical characteristics including how to properly load, unload and clear a malfunction from your gun.

- Obviously, not all guns are mechanically the same. Never assume that what applies to one make or model is exactly applicable to another.

- You should direct questions regarding the operation of your gun to your firearms dealer, or contact the manufacturer directly.

6. Store your gun safely and securely to prevent unauthorized use. Guns and ammunition should be stored separately.

- Even when the gun is not in your hands, you must still think of safety.

- Use a California-approved firearms safety device on the gun, such as a trigger lock or cable lock, so it cannot be fired.

- Store your gun unloaded in a locked container, such as a California-approved lock box or a gun safe.

- Store your gun in a different location than the ammunition.

- For maximum safety you should use both a locking device and a storage container.

The six basic safety rules are the foundational rules for gun safety. However, there are additional safety points which must not be overlooked:

- Never handle a gun when you are in an emotional state such as anger or depression. Your judgment may be impaired.

- Never shoot a gun in celebration (such as on the Fourth of July or New Year's Eve, for example). Not only is this unsafe, but it is generally illegal. A bullet fired into the air can return to the ground with enough speed to cause injury or death.

- Do not shoot at water, flat or hard surfaces. The bullet can ricochet and hit someone or something other than the target.

- Hand your gun to someone only after you verify that it is unloaded and the cylinder or action is open. Take a gun from someone only after you verify that it is unloaded and the cylinder or action is open.

- Guns, alcohol and drugs don't mix. Alcohol and drugs can negatively affect judgment as well as physical coordination. Alcohol and any other substances are likely to impair normal mental or physical functions and should not be used before or while handling guns. Avoid handling and using your gun when you are taking medications that cause drowsiness or include a warning to not operate machinery while taking the drug.

- The loud noise from a fired gun can cause hearing damage, and the debris and hot gas that is often emitted can result in eye injury. Always wear ear and eye protection when shooting a gun.

1. A safe practice when handling a gun is to rest your finger on the outside of the trigger guard or along the side of the gun until you are ready to shoot. (page 4)

   True   False

2. To "know your target, its surroundings and beyond," you must consider that if the bullet misses or completely passes through the target, it could strike a person or object. (page 5)

   True   False

3. Drinking alcohol while handling firearms is safe if your blood alcohol level remains below the legal limit. (page 6)

   True   False

4. Which of the following safety points should you remember when handling a gun? (page 6)

   A. Never shoot a gun in celebration.

   B. Do not fire at water, flat or hard surfaces.

   C. Wear ear and eye protection when shooting a gun.

   D. All of the above.

5. As a safety measure, your firearm should always be pointed: (page 4)

   A. To the north.

   B. In the safest possible direction.

   C. Up.

   D. Down.

6. One of the safety rules is to know how to properly: (page 5)

   A. Clear a malfunction.

   B. Operate your gun.

   C. Load your gun.

   D. Clean your gun.

CHAPTER 2

Firearms and Children

FIREARM OWNER RESPONSIBILITY

It is a firearm owner's responsibility to take all possible steps to make sure a child cannot gain access to firearms. In fact, this responsibility is mandated by California law. The overall abiding rule is to store your gun in a safe and responsible manner at all times. As a firearm owner, you should be aware of the laws regarding children and firearms.

Summary of Safe Storage Laws Regarding Children

You may be guilty of a misdemeanor or a felony if you keep a loaded firearm within any premises that are under your custody or control and a child under 18 years of age obtains and uses it, resulting in injury or death, or carries it to a public place, unless you stored the firearm in a locked container or locked the firearm with a locking device to temporarily keep it from functioning. Please refer to Page 42 for more specific information regarding safe storage laws related to children.

You Cannot Be Too Careful with Children and Guns

There is no such thing as being too careful with children and guns. Never assume that simply because a toddler may lack finger strength, they can't pull the trigger. A child's thumb has twice the strength of the other fingers. When a toddler's thumb "pushes" against a trigger, invariably the barrel of the gun is pointing directly at the child's face. NEVER leave a firearm lying around the house. Please refer to Pages 31 and 32 for more information regarding safe storage and methods of childproofing your firearm.

Child safety precautions still apply even if you have no children or if your children have grown to adulthood and left home. A nephew, niece, neighbor's child or a grandchild may come to visit. Practice gun safety at all times.

To prevent injury or death caused by improper storage of guns in a home where children are likely to be present, you should store all guns unloaded, lock them with a firearms safety device and store them in a locked container. Ammunition should be stored in a location separate from the gun.

Talking to Children about Guns

Children are naturally curious about things they don't know about or think are "forbidden." When a child asks questions or begins to act out "gun play," you may want to address his or her curiosity by answering the questions as honestly and openly as possible. This will remove the mystery and reduce the natural curiosity. Also, it is important to remember to talk to children in a manner they can relate to and understand. This is very important, especially when teaching children about the difference between "real" and "make-believe." Let children know that, even though they may look the same, real guns are very different than toy guns. A real gun will hurt or kill someone who is shot.

Instill a Mind Set of Safety and Responsibility

The American Academy of Pediatrics reports that adolescence is a highly vulnerable stage in life for teenagers struggling to develop traits of identity, independence and autonomy. Children, of course, are both naturally curious and innocently unaware of many dangers around them. Thus, adolescents as well as children may not be sufficiently safeguarded by cautionary words, however frequent contrary actions can completely undermine good advice. A "do as I say and not as I do" approach to gun safety is both irresponsible and dangerous.

Remember that actions speak louder than words. Children learn most by observing the adults around them. By practicing safe conduct you will also be teaching safe conduct.

RULES FOR KIDS

Adults should be aware that a child could discover a gun when a parent or any other adult is not present. This could happen in the child's own home; the home of a neighbor, friend or relative; or in a public place such as a school or park. If this should happen, a child should know the following rules and be taught to practice them.

1. Stop

The first rule for a child to follow if he/she finds or sees a gun is to stop what he/she is doing.

2. Don't Touch!

The second rule is for a child not to touch a gun he/she finds or sees. A child may think the best thing to do if he/she finds a gun is to pick it up and take it to an adult. A child needs to know he/she should NEVER touch a gun he/she may find or see.

3. Leave the Area

The third rule is to immediately leave the area. This would include never taking a gun away from another child or trying to stop someone from using gun.

4. Tell an Adult

The last rule is for a child to tell an adult about the gun he/she has seen. This includes times when other kids are playing with or shooting a gun.

Please note that, while there is no better advice at this time for children or adolescents who encounter a gun by happenstance, the California Chapter of the American College of Emergency Physicians reports that such warnings alone may be insufficient accident prevention measures with children and adolescents.

1. Toddlers lack the strength to pull the trigger of a firearm. (page 8)

   True   False

2. You may face misdemeanor or felony charges if you keep a loaded firearm where a child obtains and improperly uses it. (page 8)

   True   False

3. There is no such thing as being too careful with children and guns. (page 8)

   True   False

4. An important lesson children should learn is that guns are not toys. (page 9)

   True   False

5. The four safety "Rules for Kids" if they see a gun are: (page 9)

   A. _____

   B. _____

   C. _____

   D. _____

6. Child safety precautions only apply if you have children. (page 8)

   True   False

Answers: 1: False, 2: True, 3: True, 4: True, 5: A. Stop, B. Don't Touch, C. Leave the Area, D. Tell an Adult, 6: False

CHAPTER 3
Firearm Operation and Safe Handling

SAFE HANDLING DEMONSTRATION

Pursuant to Penal Code sections 26850 and 26860, prior to taking delivery of a firearm from a licensed firearms dealer in California, an individual must correctly perform a safe handling demonstration with the firearm he or she is acquiring. The safe handling demonstration must be performed in the presence of a DOJ Certified Instructor on or after the date the Dealer Record of Sale (DROS) is submitted to the DOJ and before the firearm is delivered. This section lists each of the steps that constitute the statutorily mandated safe handling demonstrations for the most common handgun types (semiautomatic pistols, double-action revolvers and single-action revolvers). This section also includes safe handling demonstration steps for most long gun types. However, this information will not appear on the DOJ written test on firearm safety. Please note that a dummy round as stated in this guide refers to one bright orange, red or other readily identifiable dummy round. If no readily identifiable dummy round is available, an empty cartridge casing with an empty primer pocket may be used.

The safe handling demonstration shall commence with the firearm unloaded and locked with the firearm safety device with which it is required to be delivered, if applicable. While maintaining muzzle awareness (that is, the firearm is pointed in a safe direction, preferably down at the ground) and trigger discipline (that is, the trigger finger is outside of the trigger guard and alongside of the firearm frame) at all times, the firearm recipient shall correctly and safely perform the safe handling demonstration steps for each firearm type.

REVOLVER PARTS AND OPERATION

How a Revolver Works

A revolver has a rotating cylinder containing a number of chambers. There are usually five or six chambers. The action of the trigger or hammer will line up a chamber with the barrel and firing pin. Releasing the cylinder latch allows the cylinder to swing out for loading, unloading and inspection.

Revolvers are either single or double-action. The primary difference between these two types of revolvers is the function of the trigger. On a single-action revolver the trigger has a single function to release the hammer. The trigger on a double- action revolver has two functions to cock the hammer and to release it.

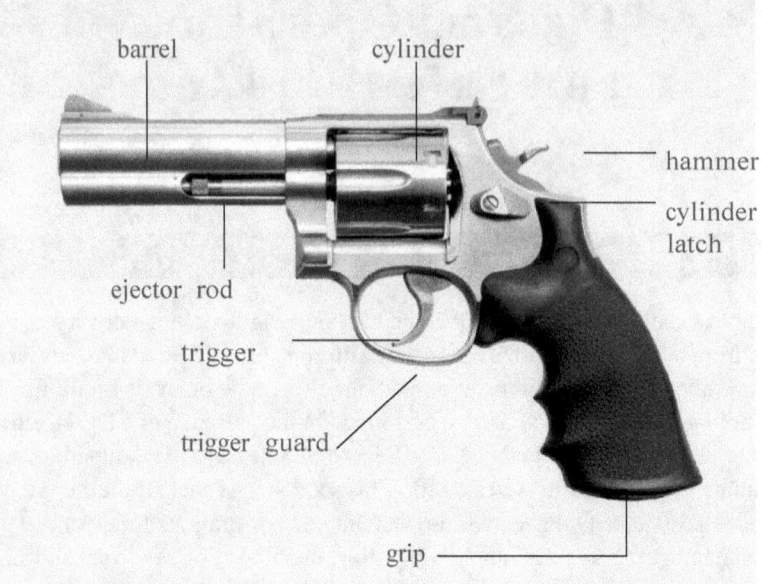

barrel   cylinder

hammer

cylinder latch

ejector rod

trigger

trigger guard

grip

1. Open the cylinder.

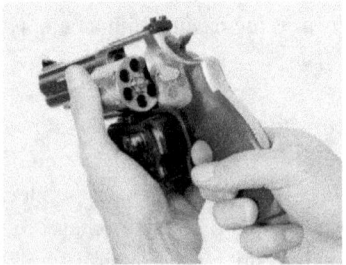

2. Visually and physically inspect each chamber to ensure that the revolver is unloaded.

3. Remove the firearm safety device. If the firearm safety device prevents any of the previous steps, remove the firearm safety device during the appropriate step.

4. While maintaining muzzle awareness and trigger discipline, load one dummy round into a chamber of the cylinder and rotate the cylinder so that the round is in the next-to-fire position.

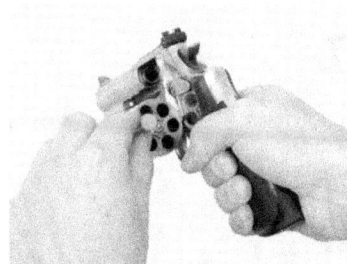

5. Close the cylinder.

6. Open the cylinder and eject the round.

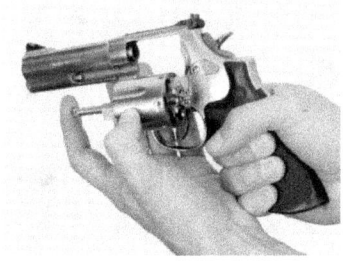

7. Visually and physically inspect each chamber to ensure that the revolver is unloaded.

8. Apply the firearm safety device, if applicable.

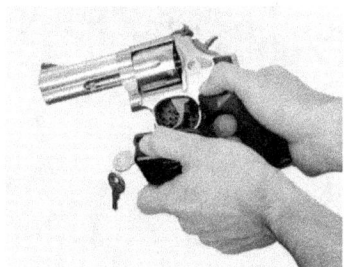

NOTE: Simply spinning a revolver to an empty chamber does not unload it or make it safe. The cylinder rotates to the next chamber before the hammer falls.

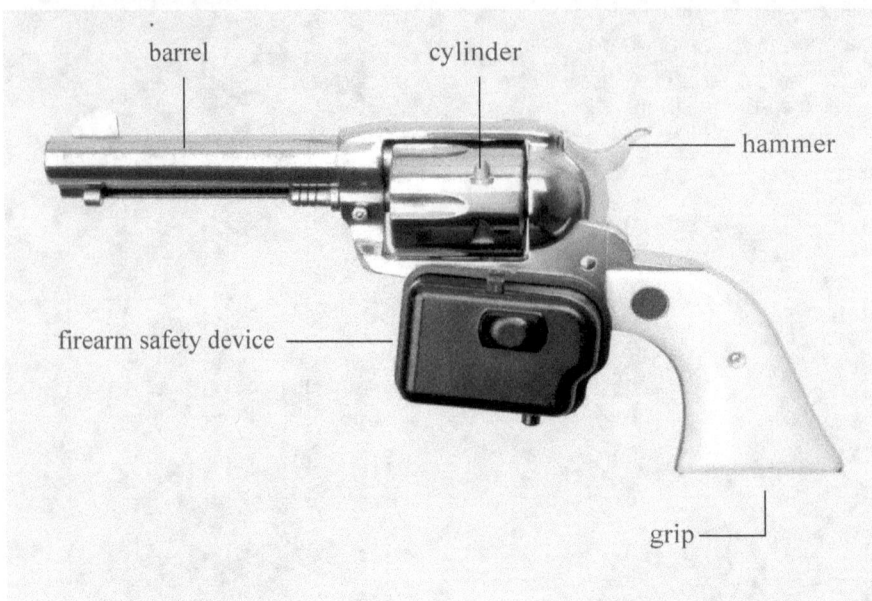

barrel

cylinder

hammer

firearm safety device

grip

1. Open the loading gate.

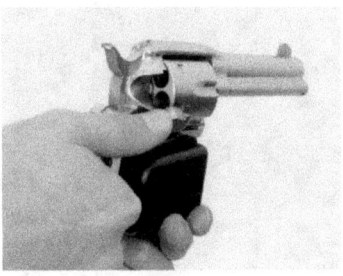

2. Visually and physically inspect each chamber to ensure that the revolver is unloaded.

3. Remove the firearm safety device required to be sold with the firearm. If the firearm safety device prevents any of the previous steps, remove the firearm safety device during the appropriate step.

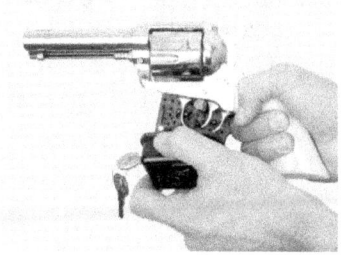

4. Load one dummy round into a chamber of the cylinder, close the loading gate and rotate the cylinder so that the round is in the next-to-fire position (the revolver may need to be placed on half-cock or the loading gate reopened).

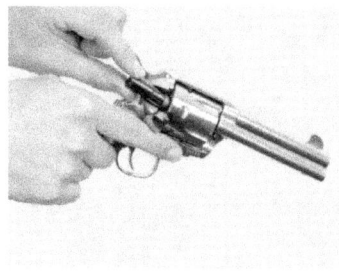

5. Open the loading gate and unload the revolver.

6. Visually and physically inspect each chamber to ensure that the revolver is unloaded.

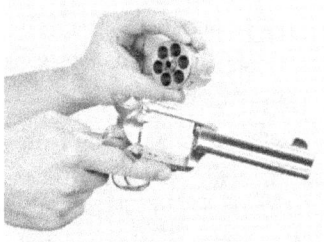

7. Apply the firearm safety device, if applicable.

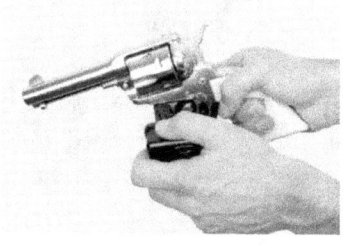

* 1873 Rule: Recipients of original versions of single-action army revolvers should be advised to carry five rounds in the cylinder and leave the chamber under the hammer empty.

How a Semiautomatic Pistol Works

A semiautomatic pistol has a single chamber. Each time the trigger is pulled, a cartridge is fired, the empty case is automatically extracted and ejected, the hammer is cocked, and a new cartridge is loaded into the chamber.

The primary difference between revolvers and semiautomatic pistols is how the ammunition is held. Revolvers use a cylinder to hold ammunition. Semiautomatic pistols use a magazine to hold ammunition. A magazine is a separate metal boxlike container into which cartridges are loaded. It is usually located within the grip. A button or catch releases the magazine.

Another difference is most semiautomatic pistols have a "safety" that is designed to prevent firing when engaged. However, it is not foolproof so do not rely on the safety to prevent an accidental discharge. A safety should be considered an additional safety measure.

Never pull the trigger on any firearm with the safety in the "safe" position because thereafter the firearm could fire at any time without the trigger ever being touched. If a firearm is dropped, it may land hard enough to activate the firing mechanism without the trigger being touched.

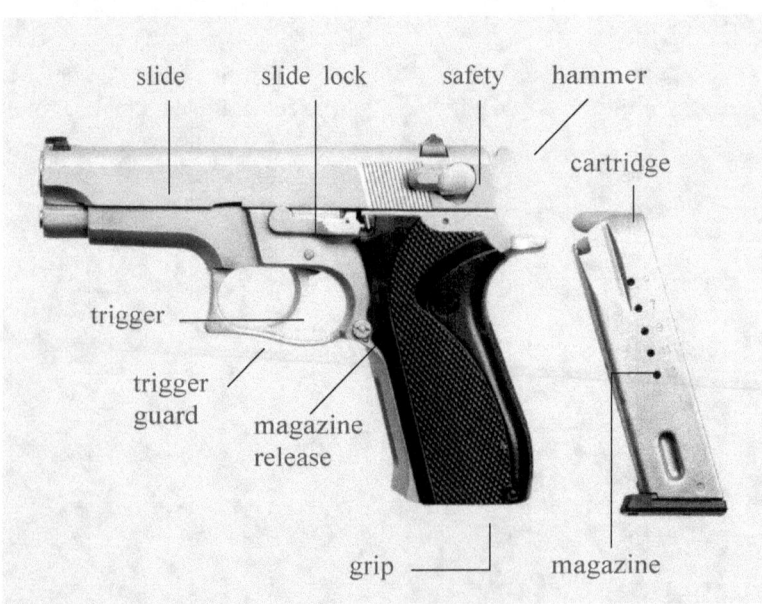

1. Remove the magazine.

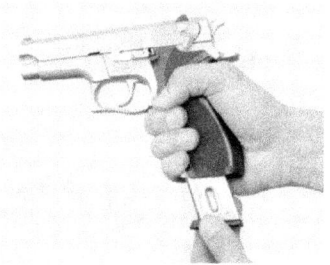

2. Lock the slide back. If the model of firearm does not allow the slide to be locked back, pull the slide back, visually and physically inspect the chamber to ensure that it is clear.

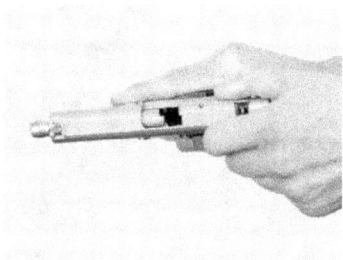

3. Visually and physically inspect the chamber, to ensure that the firearm is unloaded.

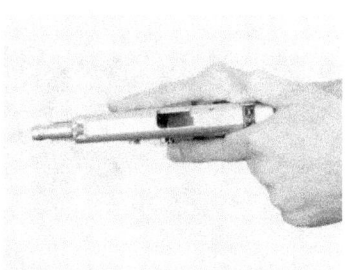

4. Remove the firearm safety device, if applicable. If the firearm safety device prevents any of the previous steps, remove the firearm safety device during the appropriate step.

5. Load one dummy round into the magazine.

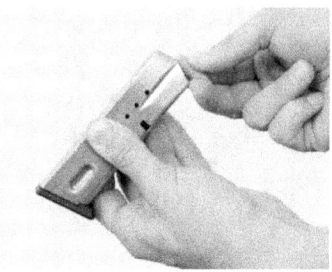

6. Insert the magazine into the magazine well of the firearm.

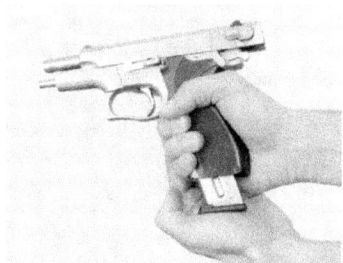

7. Manipulate the slide release or pull back and release the slide.

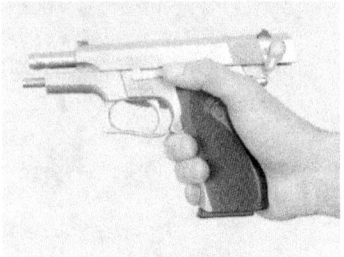

8. Remove the magazine.

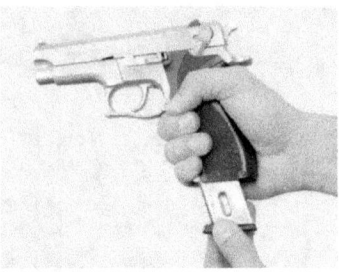

9. Visually inspect the chamber to reveal that a round can be chambered with the magazine removed.

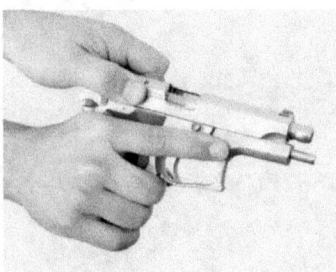

10. Lock the slide back to eject the dummy round. If the firearm is of a model that does not allow the slide to be locked back, pull the slide back and physically check the chamber to ensure that the chamber is clear.

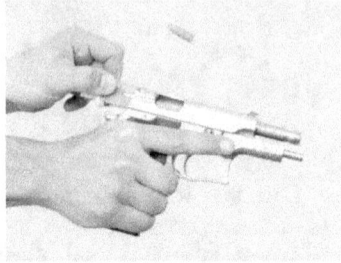

11. Apply the safety, if applicable.

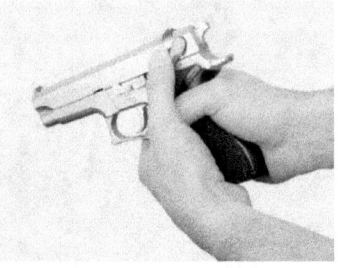

12. Apply the firearm safety device, if applicable.

Note: If you release the slide before inserting the magazine, there will NOT be a cartridge in the chamber.

You should NOT assume a semiautomatic pistol is unloaded just because the magazine is removed from the handgun.

Do not allow the slide to go forward UNLESS you have:

    1. Checked again to be sure the chamber is empty, and

    2. Checked again to be sure the magazine has been REMOVED.

If you pull the slide back ejecting the cartridge, check the chamber, let the slide go forward, and THEN remove the magazine, you have a loaded, dangerous firearm (a cartridge is in the chamber) even though you have removed the magazine. It is common and sometimes fatal to make this error.

ALWAYS REMOVE THE MAGAZINE FIRST!

The demonstration shall commence with the firearm unloaded and locked with the firearm safety device with which it is required to be delivered, if applicable. While maintaining muzzle awareness (that is, the firearm is pointed in a safe direction, preferably down at the ground) and trigger discipline (that is, the trigger finger is outside of the trigger guard and alongside of the receiver) at all times, the firearms recipient shall correctly and safely perform the steps identified for each firearm type.

The following safe handling demonstration steps for long guns are generally applicable to the various firearm models of each firearm "type" (e.g. pump action long gun, break-top revolver, etc.). However, the specified safe handling demonstration steps may not be appropriate for a particular model of firearm. If uncertain, refer to the owner's manual or consult with a DOJ Certified Instructor.

Pump Action Long Gun

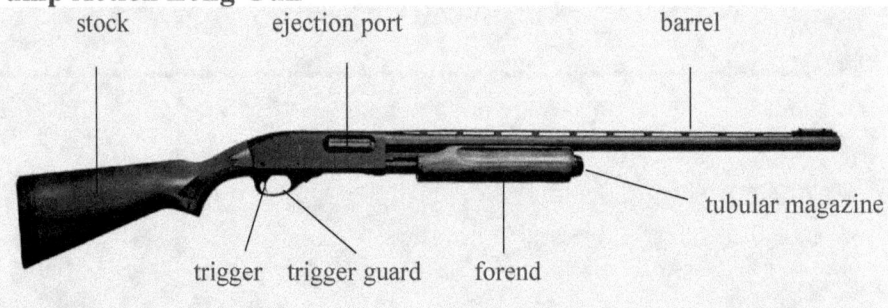

stock   ejection port   barrel

tubular magazine

trigger   trigger guard   forend

1. Open the ejection port.
2. Visually and physically inspect the chamber to ensure the firearm is unloaded. Visually and physically inspect the magazine follower to ensure the magazine is unloaded (if the magazine follower is not visible, there may be shotshells or cartridges lodged in the tubular magazine).
3. Remove the firearm safety device. If the firearm safety device prevents any of the previous steps, remove the firearm safety device during the appropriate step.
4. While maintaining muzzle awareness and trigger discipline, load one dummy round into the magazine loading port.
5. Pull the forend (or forearm) rearward toward the receiver causing the dummy round to enter the breech. Push the forend forward to chamber the round. The dummy round should have moved from the tubular magazine into the chamber.
6. Push the action (carrier) release button and again pull the forend toward the receiver causing the action to open. The dummy round should extract from the chamber and be ejected through the ejection port.
7. Engage the safety.
8. Apply the firearm safety device, if applicable.

Break-Top Long Gun

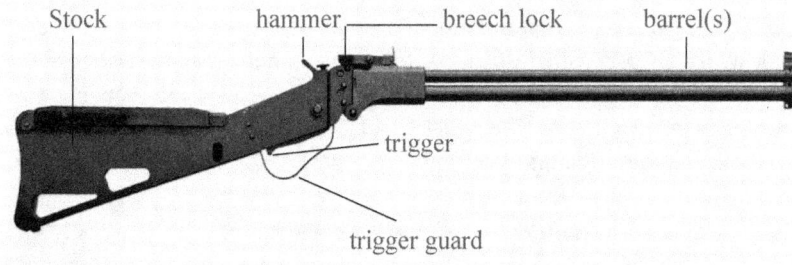

1. Open the breech.
2. Visually and physically inspect the chamber/barrel to ensure the firearm is unloaded.
3. Remove the firearm safety device. If the firearm safety device prevents any of the previous steps, remove the firearm safety device during the appropriate step.
4. While maintaining muzzle awareness and trigger discipline, load one dummy round into a barrel.
5. Close and lock the action.
6. Unlock and open the action.
7. Remove the dummy round.
8. Apply the firearm safety device, if applicable.

Bolt Action Long Gun

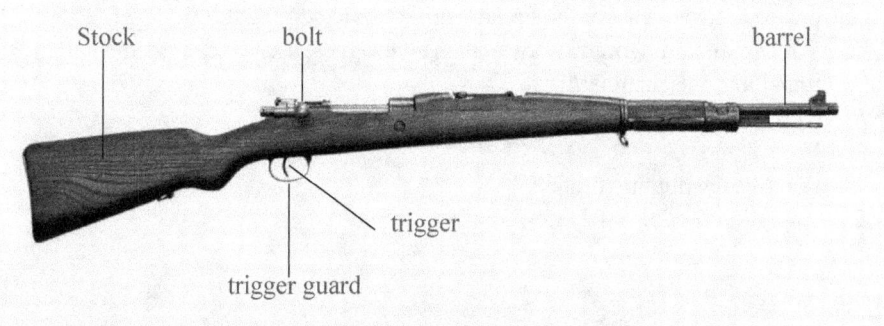

1. Visually and physically inspect the chamber/barrel to ensure the long gun is unloaded. Also visually and physically inspect the internal magazine to ensure it is unloaded.
2. Remove the firearm safety device. If the firearm safety device prevents any of the previous steps, remove the firearm safety device during the appropriate step.
3. While maintaining muzzle awareness and trigger discipline, load one dummy round into the chamber/barrel.
4. Close and lock the action.
5. Unlock and open the action.
6. Remove the dummy round.
7. Apply the firearm safety device, if applicable.

Lever Action Long Gun

When handling a lever action firearm with an exposed hammer, please use caution and consult with a DOJ Certified Instructor for proper handling steps. Use only flat point, hollow point, round nose flat point, or similar rounds. Never use pointed or conical point rounds in a center fire rifle with a tubular magazine. Failure to follow these instructions may result in injury to yourself or others, or cause damage to your firearm.

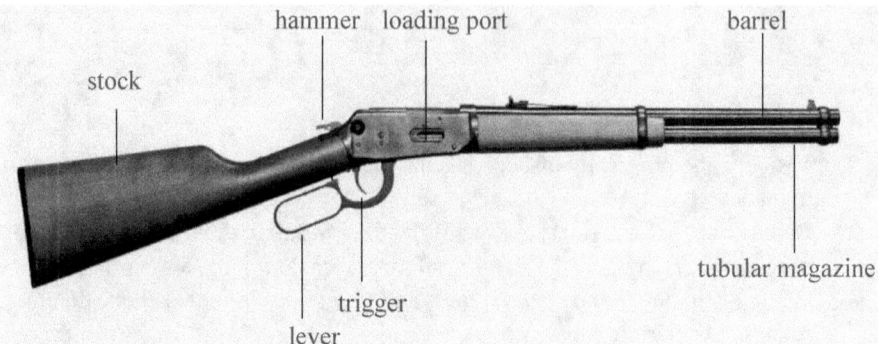

1. Open the breech.
2. Visually and physically inspect the chamber/barrel to ensure the firearm is unloaded. Visually and physically inspect the magazine follower to ensure the magazine is unloaded (if the magazine follower is not visible, there may be cartridges lodged in the tubular magazine).
3. Remove the firearm safety device. If the firearm safety device prevents any of the previous steps, remove the firearm safety device during the appropriate step.
4. While maintaining muzzle awareness and trigger discipline, load one dummy round into the chamber/barrel.
5. Close and lock the action.
6. Unlock and open the action.
7. Remove the dummy round.
8. Apply the firearm safety device, if applicable.

Semiautomatic Long Gun With a Detachable Magazine

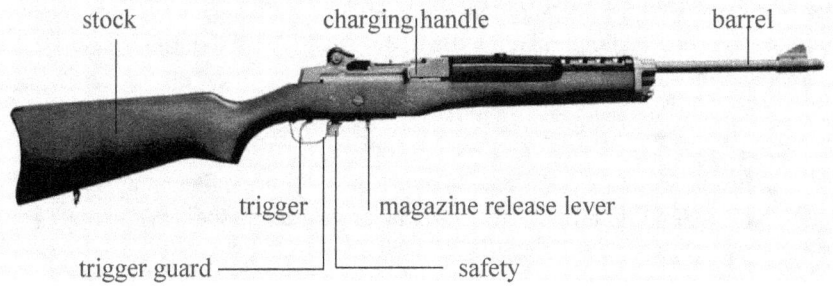

stock   charging handle   barrel

trigger   magazine release lever

trigger guard ——— safety

1. Remove the magazine.
2. Pull the bolt back and lock it open if possible.
3. Visually and physically inspect the barrel/chamber to ensure the firearm is unloaded.
4. Remove the firearm safety device. If the firearm safety device prevents any of the previous steps, remove the firearm safety device during the appropriate step.
5. While maintaining muzzle awareness and trigger discipline, load one dummy round into the magazine.
6. Insert the magazine into the magazine well.
7. Close and lock the action.
8. Unlock and open the action.
9. Remove the dummy round.
10. Apply the firearm safety device, if applicable.

Semiautomatic Long Gun With a Fixed Magazine

stock   operating rod   barrel

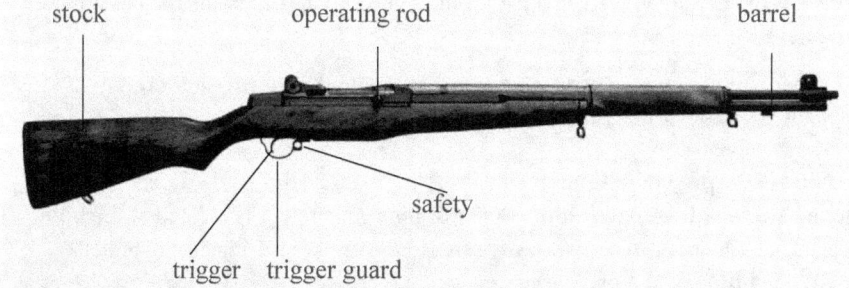

safety

trigger   trigger guard

1. Pull the bolt back and lock it open if possible.
2. Visually and physically inspect the barrel/chamber to ensure the firearm is unloaded. Also visually and physically inspect the internal magazine to ensure it is unloaded.
3. Remove the firearm safety device. If the firearm safety device prevents any of the previous steps, remove the firearm safety device during the appropriate step.
4. While maintaining muzzle awareness and trigger discipline, load one dummy round into the magazine.
5. Close and lock the action.
6. Unlock and open the action.
7. Remove the dummy round (the dummy round should have extracted from the chamber and ejected from the breech).

AMMUNITION

An often overlooked aspect of safe firearm operation is knowing about the ammunition you use. It is important for you to know which ammunition can be used safely in your firearm.

Ammunition Components

A firearm cartridge, commonly referred to as a "round," is a single unit of ammunition made up of four parts: the case, the primer, the propellant and the bullet.

Components of a Cartridge

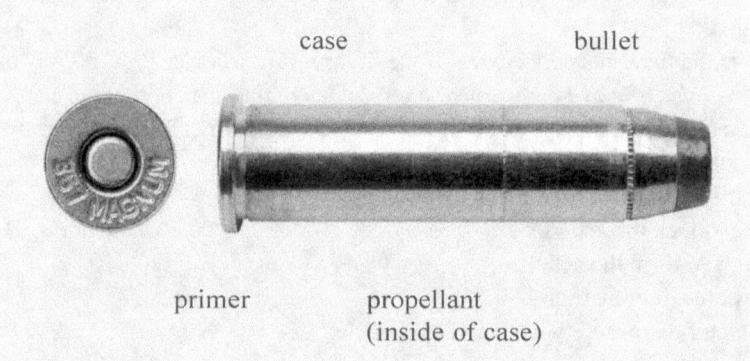

case   bullet

primer   propellant
(inside of case)

The case is the metal cylinder that is closed at one end and contains the other three components.

The primer is the impact-sensitive chemical compound used for ignition. The propellant is a fast-burning chemical compound.

The bullet is the projectile fired from a firearm. It is usually made of lead, sometimes covered with a layer of copper or other metal and is located at the tip of the cartridge. People often mistakenly refer to the entire cartridge as a "bullet." Actually the bullet is just one part of a cartridge.

PHYSICS OF GUNFIRE

To understand the power of a firearm, it is helpful to know some of the physics of gunfire. The fall of the hammer causes the primer to ignite the powder, which burns to produce gases. These rapidly-expanding gases push the bullet through the barrel and toward the target. The push of gases against the firearm results in what is called recoil. Some shooters are startled by recoil. Firearms vary in how much recoil they generate. Anticipation of recoil may cause an inexperienced shooter to grasp the firearm too tightly or flinch. Shooting a firearm properly minimizes the negative effects of recoil on the shooter.

FIREARM AND AMMUNITION CALIBERS

Firearms and ammunition are made in various calibers. Firearm caliber refers to barrel diameter. Revolvers generally have the caliber information on the barrel. Semiautomatic pistols generally have the caliber information on the slide. Ammunition caliber refers to bullet diameter. Ammunition has the caliber information on the box. Some of the more common calibers are the .22, .45, and 9 mm. You must only use the caliber of ammunition recommended by the manufacturer of your firearm.

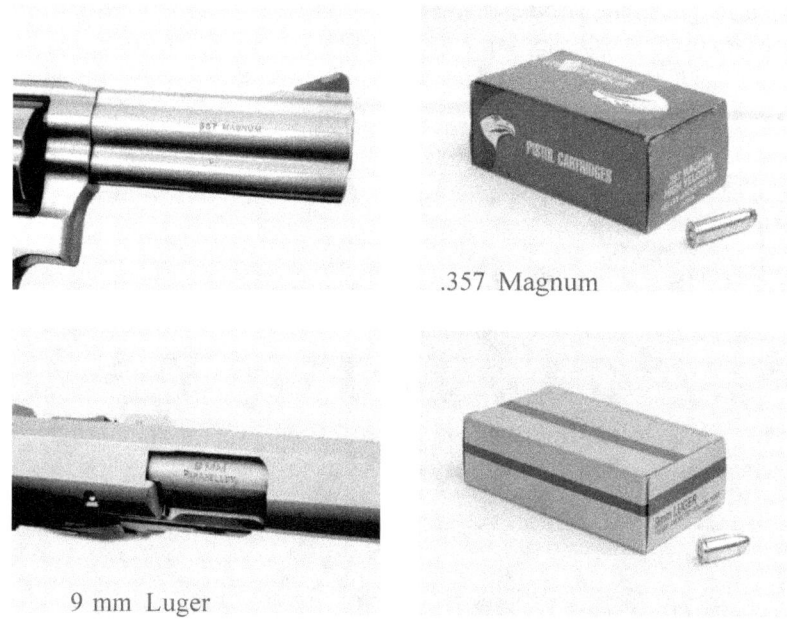

.357 Magnum

9 mm Luger

Just because a cartridge fits your firearm does not necessarily mean the cartridge is safe to shoot. A firearm may not be able to handle the pressure created by using incorrect ammunition. This could result in damage to the firearm and possible injury to yourself or bystanders.

Never shoot ammunition that is old, dirty, corroded or wet, or ammunition that cannot be fully identified. This could cause a malfunction such as a jam or a misfire, or explosion of the firearm. Never throw ammunition in the trash. Call your local refuse department and ask for proper disposal instructions.

Some ammunition is illegal. Your firearms dealer can help you identify the correct and legal ammunition for your firearm. Purchase your ammunition from an authorized ammunition dealer only.

DANGEROUS RANGE

In order to shoot a firearm safely, you need to know not only your target but also the dangerous range of your ammunition. The dangerous range is the distance that a bullet can travel. Most ammunition can travel at least a mile, with some having the capability of traveling MORE than two miles. Therefore, even though you may fire at a target only a few feet or yards away, your bullet could travel far beyond your target. As it travels, the potential for damage widens. The importance of the dangerous range is that you must consider how much farther the bullet can travel beyond the target because a bullet that misses or passes through a target could strike a person or object. If you think only of your target and not the dangerous range, you might mistakenly think someone or something is 'too far away' to be in danger.

Another important point to remember is that most ammunition can easily penetrate the interior walls of a house and still travel some distance before losing its energy. High velocity or magnum ammunition has even greater penetration and distance capabilities.

Remember: Once you fire, you are responsible for any damage or injury your bullet causes.

MALFUNCTIONS

Any machine can malfunction. A firearm is no different. If your firearm malfunctions, always keep the basic safety rules in mind and do the following:

C A U T I O N	STOP FIRING! KEEP THE GUN POINTED IN A SAFE DIRECTION. WAIT TEN SECONDS. SEEK COMPETENT HELP.

If you are at a range, the usual procedure to follow when a malfunction occurs is to keep your firearm pointed down range, keep your finger off the trigger and raise your non-shooting hand until a range official arrives. You have a potentially dangerous situation!

1. The importance of the "dangerous range" is that a bullet can travel far beyond the intended target. (page 27)

   True   False

2. The safety on a semiautomatic pistol is not foolproof. (page 17)

   True   False

3. Just because a cartridge fits into your firearm does not necessarily mean it is safe to shoot. (page 26)

   True   False

4. In the case of a malfunction, you should: (page 27)

   A. Keep your finger on the trigger.
   B. Immediately drop the firearm.
   C. Try and determine where the malfunction is.
   D. Keep the gun pointed in a safe direction.

5. After ensuring a double-action revolver is pointed in a safe direction and with your finger off the trigger, you begin unloading the firearm by: (page 13)

   A. Opening the cylinder.
   B. Locking the slide back.
   C. Opening the loading gate.
   D. Pushing the magazine release.

6. Firearm or ammunition caliber refers to: (page 26)

   A. Barrel length.
   B. Magazine capacity.
   C. Barrel or bullet diameter.
   D. Bullet velocity.

7. A magazine is part of a: (page 17)

   A. Single-action revolver.
   B. Double-action revolver.
   C. Semiautomatic pistol.
   D. Single-action and a double-action revolver.

Answers: 1: True, 2: True, 3: True, 4: D, 5: A, 6: C, 7: C

CHAPTER 4
Firearm Ownership

UNDERSTAND THE SAFETY ASPECTS OF YOUR FIREARM

Get advice from a professional sales person on the safety aspects of the firearm you are considering buying. Select the firearm that best suits your personal needs. Ask a lot of questions! Ask about the correct ammunition for the firearm you have selected.

Become thoroughly familiar with the mechanics of the firearm you have selected. By knowing exactly how your firearm works, you are more likely to recognize any possible safety problems.

CAREFULLY READ ALL INSTRUCTIONAL MATERIAL

An owner's manual from the manufacturer of your firearm should be provided when you buy a new firearm. Manuals for used firearms usually can be obtained by writing or calling the manufacturer.

Carefully read the manual and use it to familiarize yourself with the firearm and its operation.

ENROLL IN A FIREARM TRAINING COURSE

To help you learn to drive a car you probably had some "behind the wheel" training and practice before you got your driver's license. This also applies to firearm ownership. The best way to become skilled in using and understanding how your firearm operates is to enroll in a "hands-on" training course. There are many firearm training courses that can provide additional safety information.

For information on training courses in your area, contact a local firearms dealer or firearms safety organization.

CLEANING AND REPAIR

Maintenance is part of being a responsible firearms owner. Firearms should be cleaned regularly and especially after prolonged storage. The barrel should be cleaned after every use. Accumulated moisture, dirt or grease can interfere with the efficient and safe operation of a firearm.

Firearm cleaning kits and materials can be purchased from most firearms dealers. Be aware that some firearm cleaning substances are toxic. Carefully read and follow the instructions on the cleaning products.

You should clean your firearm in a location where you will have no distractions. Before you begin, always make sure your firearm is unloaded and remove any ammunition from the cleaning area. Accidents can happen if cleaning procedures are not followed correctly and safely. Therefore, you should follow the cleaning instructions in your owner's manual and on your cleaning products. Firearms dealers or gunsmiths also are good sources for cleaning information.

Care should be taken to ensure adequate ventilation at all times to reduce the risk of inhaling lead particles. To avoid accidental ingestion of lead particles, never handle food or drink without first washing your hands. Do not smoke when exposed to lead. Wash your hands thoroughly after exposure.

Periodically inspect all firearms you own to be sure that they are in good working condition. If you notice any problems, have your firearm checked by a competent gunsmith. Any repairs should be made only by a gunsmith or the manufacturer of the firearm. You should not attempt to make any major modifications to your firearm. Some modifications are illegal and dangerous. They also could void the manufacturer's warranty.

By keeping your firearm properly maintained, you will ensure that it is safe to operate and will function reliably for many years.

SAFETY AND STORAGE DEVICES

If you decide to keep a firearm in your home you must consider the issue of how to store the firearm in a safe and secure manner. California recognizes the importance of safe storage by requiring that all firearms sold in California be accompanied by a DOJ-approved firearms safety device or proof that the purchaser owns a gun safe that meets regulatory standards established by the DOJ. The current list of DOJ-approved firearms safety devices and the gun safe standards can be viewed at the following DOJ website: http://oag.ca.gov/firearms/fsdcertlist.

There are a variety of safety and storage devices currently available to the public in a wide range of prices. Some devices are locking mechanisms designed to keep the firearm from being loaded or fired, but don't prevent the firearm from being handled or stolen. There are also locking storage containers that hold the firearm out of sight. For maximum safety you should use both a firearm safety device and a locking storage container to store your unloaded firearm.

Two of the most common locking mechanisms are trigger locks and cable locks. Trigger locks are typically two-piece devices that fit around the trigger and trigger guard to prevent access to the trigger. One side has a post that fits into a hole in the other side. They are locked by a key or combination locking mechanism. Cable locks typically work by looping a strong steel cable through the action of the firearm to block the firearm's operation and prevent accidental firing. However, neither trigger locks nor cable locks are designed to prevent access to the firearm.

Smaller lock boxes and larger gun safes are two of the most common types of locking storage containers. One advantage of lock boxes and gun safes is that they are designed to completely prevent unintended handling and removal of a firearm. Lock boxes are generally constructed of sturdy, high-grade metal opened by either a key or combination lock. Gun safes are quite heavy, usually weighing at least 50 pounds. While gun safes are typically the most expensive firearm storage devices, they are generally more reliable and secure.

Remember: Safety and storage devices are only as secure as the precautions you take to protect the key or combination to the lock.

METHODS OF CHILDPROOFING

As a responsible firearm owner, you need to be aware of the methods of childproofing your firearm, whether or not you have children.

Whenever children could be around, whether your own, or a friend's, relative's or neighbor's, additional safety steps should be taken when storing firearms and ammunition in your home.

- Always store your firearm unloaded.
- Use a firearms safety device AND store the firearm in a locked container.
- Store the ammunition separately in a locked container.

Always storing your firearm securely is the best method of childproofing your firearm; however, your choice of a storage place can add another element of safety. Carefully choose the storage place in your home especially if children may be around.

- Do not store your firearm where it is visible.
- Do not store your firearm in a bedside table, under your mattress or pillow, or on a closet shelf.
- Do not store your firearm among your valuables (such as jewelry or cameras) unless it is locked in a secure container.
- Make sure the location you store your firearm and ammunition is not easily accessible to children.
- Consider storing firearms not possessed for self-defense in a safe and secure manner away from the home.

1. It is important to carefully read all instructional material you receive with your firearm. (page 29)

   True   False

2. Certain modifications, when made to a firearm, may void its warranty. (page 30)

   True   False

3. It is safe to store a loaded firearm in your bedside table. (page 32)

   True   False

4. Two common firearms safety devices are trigger locks and cable locks. (page 31)

   True   False

5. Which of the following steps should be taken to "childproof" your firearm? (page 32)

   A. Use a firearms safety device AND store the firearm in a locked container.

   B. Always store your firearm unloaded.

   C. Store ammunition separately in a locked container.

   D. All of the above.

Answers: 1: True, 2: True, 3: False, 4: True, 5: D

Prohibited Firearms Transfers and Straw Purchases

What is a straw purchase?

A straw purchase is buying a gun for someone who is prohibited by law from possessing one, or buying a gun for someone who does not want his or her name associated with the transaction.

It is a violation of California law for a person who is not licensed as a California firearms dealer to transfer a firearm to another unlicensed person, without conducting such a transfer through a licensed firearms dealer. (Pen. Code, § 27545.) Such a transfer may be punishable as a felony. (Pen. Code, § 27590.)

Furthermore, it is a violation of federal law to either (1) make a false or fictitious statement on an application to purchase a firearm about a material fact, such as the identity of the person who ultimately will acquire the firearm (commonly known as "lying and buying") (18 U.S.C. 922(a)(6)), or (2) knowingly transfer a firearm to a person who is prohibited by federal law from possessing and purchasing it. (18 U.S.C. 922(d).) Such transfers are punishable under federal law by a $250,000 fine and 10 years in federal prison. (18 U.S.C. 924(a)(2).)

Things to remember about prohibited firearms transfers and straw purchases:

An illegal firearm purchase (straw purchase) is a federal crime.

An illegal firearm purchase can bring a felony conviction sentence of 10 years in jail and a fine of up to $250,000.

Buying a gun and giving it to someone who is prohibited from owning one is a state and federal crime.

Never buy a gun for someone who is prohibited by law or unable to do so.

CHAPTER 5

Firearms Laws

INTRODUCTION TO THE LAWS

As the owner of a firearm, it is your responsibility to understand and comply with all federal, state and local laws regarding firearms ownership. Many of the laws described below pertain to the possession, use and storage of firearms in the home and merit careful review. This section contains a general summary of the state laws that govern the use of firearms, particularly handguns, by persons other than law enforcement officers or members of the armed forces. It is not designed to provide individual guidance for specific situations, nor does it address federal or local laws. Persons having specific questions are encouraged to seek legal advice from an attorney, or consult their local law enforcement agency, local prosecutor or law library.

SALES AND TRANSFERS OF FIREARMS

In California, only licensed California firearms dealers are authorized to engage in retail sales of firearms. These retail sales require the purchaser to provide personal identifier information for the Dealers' Record of Sale (DROS) document that the firearms dealer must submit to the DOJ. There is a mandatory 10-day waiting period before the firearms dealer can deliver the firearm to the purchaser. During this 10-day waiting period, the DOJ conducts a firearms eligibility background check to ensure the purchaser is not prohibited from lawfully possessing firearms. Although there are exceptions, generally all firearms purchasers must be at least 18 years of age to purchase a long gun (rifle or shotgun) and 21 years of age to purchase a handgun (pistol or revolver). Additionally, purchasers must be California residents with a valid driver's license or identification card issued by the California Department of Motor Vehicles.

Generally, it is illegal for any person who is not a California licensed firearms dealer (private party) to sell or transfer a firearm to another non-licensed person (private party) unless the sale is completed through a licensed California firearms dealer. "Private party transfers" can be conducted at any licensed California firearms dealership that sells firearms. The buyer and seller must complete the required DROS document in person at the licensed firearms dealership and deliver the firearm to the dealer who will retain possession of the firearm during the mandatory 10-day waiting period. In addition to the applicable state fees, the firearms dealer may charge a fee not to exceed $10 per firearm for conducting the private party transfer.

The infrequent transfer of firearms between immediate family members is exempt from the law requiring private party transfers to be conducted through a licensed firearms dealer. For purposes of this exemption, "immediate family" means parent and child, and grandparent and grandchild, but does not include other types of transfers, such as between brother and sister. Please note that the transferee must comply with the FSC requirement described below, prior to taking possession of the firearm. Within 30 days of the transfer, the transferee must also submit a report of the transaction to the DOJ. The required report form (Firearm Ownership Record BOF 4542A) can be downloaded from the DOJ's website at http://oag.ca.gov/firearms/forms.

The reclaiming of a pawned firearm is subject to the DROS and 10-day waiting period requirements.

Proof-of-Residency Requirement

To purchase a handgun in California you must present documentation indicating that you are a California resident. Acceptable documentation includes a utility bill from within the last three months, a signed residential lease, a property deed or military permanent duty station orders indicating assignment within California. The address provided on the DROS must match either the address on the proof-of-residency document or the address on the purchaser's California Driver license or Identification Card. (Pen. Code, § 26845.)

Firearm Safety Certificate Requirement

To purchase or acquire a firearm, you must have a valid FSC. To obtain an FSC, you must score at least 75% on an objective written test pertaining to firearms laws and safety requirements. The test is administered by DOJ Certified Instructors, who are generally located at firearms dealerships. An FSC is valid for five years. The fee for taking the FSC test and being issued an FSC is twenty-five dollars ($25). Firearms being returned to their owners, such as pawn returns, are exempt from this requirement. In the event of a lost, stolen or destroyed FSC, the issuing DOJ Certified Instructor will issue a replacement FSC for a fee of $5. You must present proof of identity to receive a replacement FSC. (Pen. Code, §§ 31610-31670.)

Safe Handling Demonstration Requirement

Prior to taking delivery of a firearm, you must successfully perform a safe handling demonstration with the firearm being purchased or acquired. Safe handling demonstrations must be performed in the presence of a DOJ Certified Instructor sometime between the date the DROS is submitted to the DOJ and the delivery of the firearm, and are generally performed at the firearms dealership. The purchaser, firearms dealer and DOJ Certified Instructor must sign an affidavit stating the safe handling demonstration was completed. The steps required to complete the safe handling demonstration for most firearm types is described in Chapter 3. Pawn returns and intra-familial transfers are not subject to the safe handling demonstration requirement. (Pen. Code, § 26850.)

Firearms Safety Device Requirement

All firearms (long guns and handguns) purchased in California must be accompanied with a firearms safety device (FSD) that has passed required safety and functionality tests and is listed on the DOJ's official roster of DOJ-approved firearms safety devices. The current roster of certified FSDs is available on the Bureau of Firearms website at http://oag.ca.gov/firearms/fsdcertlist. The FSD requirement also can be satisfied if the purchaser signs an affidavit declaring ownership of either a DOJ-approved lock box or a gun safe capable of accommodating the firearm being purchased. Pawn returns and intra-familial transfers are not subject to the FSD requirement. (Pen. Code, §§ 23635-23690.)

Roster of Handguns Certified for Sale in California

No handgun may be sold by a firearms dealer to the public unless it is of a make and model that has passed required safety and functionality tests and is listed on the DOJ's official roster of handguns certified for sale in California. The current roster of handguns certified for sale in California is available on the Bureau of Firearms website at http://certguns.doj.ca.gov. Private party transfers, intra-familial transfers, and pawn/consignment returns are exempt from this requirement. (Pen. Code, § 32000.)

One-Handgun-per-Thirty-Days Requirement

No person shall make an application to purchase more than one handgun within any 30-day period. Exemptions to the one-handgun-per-thirty-days requirement include pawn returns, intra-familial transfers and private party transfers. (Pen. Code, § 27540.)

Firearm Sales and Transfer Requirements

	Retail Sales	Private Party Transfers	Intra-familial Transfers	Pawn Returns
Proof-of-Residency Requirement (handguns)	Yes	Yes	No	Yes
Proof-of-Residency Requirement (long guns)*	No	No	No	No
Firearm Safety Certificate Requirement	Yes	Yes	Yes	No
Safe Handling Demonstration Requirement	Yes	Yes	No	No
Firearms Safety Device Requirement	Yes	Yes	No	No
Roster of Handguns Certified for sale in California	Yes	No	No	No
One Handgun Per 30 Days Requirement	Yes	No	No	No

*Federal requirements may apply.

37

Persons who move to California with the intention of establishing residency in this state must either report ownership of firearms to the DOJ within 60 days, or sell or transfer the firearm(s) pursuant to California law. (Pen. Code, § 28050.) Persons who want to keep their firearms must submit a New Resident Firearm Ownership Report, along with a $19 fee, to the DOJ. Forms are available at licensed firearms dealers, the Department of Motor Vehicles or on-line at the Bureau of Firearms web site at http://oag.ca.gov/firearms/forms. (Pen. Code, § 27560.)

CARRYING A CONCEALED WEAPON

Carrying a Concealed Handgun Without a License on One's Person or in a Vehicle

It is illegal for any person to carry a handgun concealed upon his or her person or concealed in a vehicle without a license issued pursuant to Penal Code section 26150. (Pen. Code, § 25400.) A firearm locked in a motor vehicle's trunk or in a locked container carried in the vehicle other than in the utility or glove compartment is not considered concealed within the meaning of the Penal Code section 25400; neither is a firearm carried within a locked container directly to or from a motor vehicle for any lawful purpose. (Pen. Code, § 25610.)

The prohibition from carrying a concealed handgun does not apply to licensed hunters or fishermen while engaged in hunting or fishing, or while going to or returning from the hunting expedition. (Pen. Code, § 25640.) Notwithstanding this exception for hunters or fishermen, these individuals may not carry or transport loaded firearms when going to or from the expedition. The unloaded firearms should be transported in the trunk of the vehicle or in a locked container other than the utility or glove compartment. (Pen. Code, § 25610.)

There are also occupational exceptions to the prohibition from carrying a concealed weapon, including authorized employees while engaged in specified activities. (Pen. Code, §§ 25630 & 25640.)

Licenses to Carry Concealed Weapons

A license to carry a concealed handgun or other firearm may be granted by the sheriff of the county in which the applicant resides, or the chief of the city police department of the city in which the applicant resides. Such licenses are issued only after finding that the applicant is of good moral character, that good cause exists for such a license and the applicant is not prohibited from possessing firearms. (Pen. Code, § 26150.)

Where the population of the county is less than 200,000 persons, the licensing authority may issue a license to carry a pistol, revolver or other firearm capable of being concealed upon the person, loaded and exposed. (Pen. Code, § 26150.)

Unless otherwise restricted, a license is valid throughout the state.

FIREARMS ABOARD COMMON CARRIERS

Federal and state laws generally prohibit a person from carrying any firearm or ammunition aboard any commercial passenger airplane. Similar restrictions may apply to other common carriers such as trains, ships and buses. Persons who need to carry firearms or ammunition on a common carrier should always consult the carrier in advance to determine conditions under which firearms may be transported.

FIREARMS IN THE HOME, BUSINESS OR AT THE CAMPSITE

Unless otherwise unlawful, any person over the age of 18 who is not prohibited from possessing firearms may have a loaded or unloaded firearm at his or her place of residence, temporary residence, campsite or on private property owned or lawfully possessed by the person. Any person engaged in lawful business (including nonprofit organizations) or any officer, employee or agent authorized for lawful purposes connected with the business may have a loaded firearm within the place of business if that person is over 18 years of age and not otherwise prohibited from possessing firearms. (Pen. Code, §§ 25605 & 26035.)

NOTE: If a person's place of business, residence, temporary residence, campsite or private property is located within an area where possession of a firearm is prohibited by local or federal laws, such laws would prevail.

THE USE OF LETHAL FORCE IN SELF-DEFENSE

The question of whether use of lethal force is justified in self-defense cannot be reduced to a simple list of factors. This section is based on the instructions generally given to the jury in a criminal case where self-defense is claimed and illustrates the general rules regarding the use of lethal force in self-defense.

Permissible Use of Lethal Force in Defense of Life and Body

The killing of one person by another may be justifiable when necessary to resist the attempt to commit a forcible and life-threatening crime, provided that a reasonable person in the same or similar situation would believe that (a) the person killed intended to commit a forcible and life-threatening crime; (b) there was imminent danger of such crime being accomplished; and (c) the person acted under the belief that such force was necessary to save himself or herself or another from death or a forcible and life-threatening crime. Murder, mayhem, rape and robbery are examples of forcible and life-threatening crimes. (Pen. Code, § 197.)

Limitations on the Use of Force in Self-Defense

The right of self-defense ceases when there is no further danger from an assailant. Thus, where a person attacked under circumstances initially justifying self-defense renders the attacker incapable of inflicting further injuries, the law of self-defense ceases and no further force may be used. Furthermore, a person may only use the amount of force, up to deadly force, as a reasonable person in the same or similar circumstances would believe necessary to prevent imminent injury. It is important to note the use of excessive force to counter an assault may result in civil or criminal penalties.

The right of self-defense is not initially available to a person who assaults another. However, if such a person attempts to stop further combat and clearly informs the adversary of his or her desire for peace but the opponent nevertheless continues the fight, the right of self-defense returns and is the same as the right of any other person being assaulted.

LOADED FIREARMS IN PUBLIC

It is illegal to carry a loaded firearm on one's person or in a vehicle while in any public place, on any public street, or in any place where it is unlawful to discharge a firearm. (Pen. Code, § 25850, subd. (a).)

It is illegal for the driver of any motor vehicle, or the owner of any motor vehicle irrespective of whether the owner is occupying the vehicle to knowingly permit any person to carry a loaded firearm into the vehicle in violation of Penal Code section 25850, or Fish and Game Code section 2006. (Pen. Code, § 26100.) Also, see "Miscellaneous Prohibited Acts" on next page.

In order to determine whether a firearm is loaded, peace officers are authorized to examine any firearm carried by anyone on his or her person or in a vehicle while in any public place, on any public street or in any prohibited area of an unincorporated territory. Refusal to allow a peace officer to inspect a firearm pursuant to these provisions is, in itself, grounds for arrest. (Pen. Code, § 25850, subd. (b).)

The prohibition from carrying a loaded firearm in public does not apply to any person while hunting in an area where possession and hunting is otherwise lawful or while practice shooting at target ranges. (Pen. Code, §§ 26005 & 26040.)

There are also occupational exceptions to the prohibition from carrying a loaded firearm in public, including authorized employees while engaged in specified activities. (Pen. Code, §§ 26015 & 26030.)

LARGE-CAPACITY MAGAZINES

It is generally illegal to manufacture, offer for sale, give, lend, buy, or receive any large-capacity magazine or any large-capacity conversion kit that is capable of converting an ammunition feeding device into a large-capacity magazine. (Pen. Code, §§ 32310 & 32311.)

FIREARM STORAGE DURING PROHIBITION

A person who is prohibited from owning or possessing a firearm can transfer his or her firearm(s) to a licensed firearms dealer for storage for the duration of the prohibition, provided the prohibition will end on a date specified in a court order. (Pen. Code, § 29830.)

Obliteration or Alteration of Firearm Identification

It is illegal for any person to obliterate or alter the identification marks placed on any firearm including the make, model, serial number or any distinguishing mark lawfully assigned by the owner or by the DOJ. (Pen. Code, § 23900.)

It is illegal for any person to buy, sell or possess a firearm knowing its identification has been obliterated or altered. (Pen. Code, § 23920.)

Openly Carrying an Unloaded Handgun

It is generally illegal for any person to carry upon his or her person or in a vehicle, an exposed and unloaded handgun while in or on:

- A public place or public street in an incorporated city or city and county; or
- A public street in a prohibited area of an unincorporated city or city and county. (Pen. Code, § 26350.)

Unauthorized Possession of a Firearm on School Grounds

It is illegal for any unauthorized person to possess or bring a firearm upon the grounds of, or into, any public school, including the campuses of the University of California, California State University campuses, California community colleges, any private school (kindergarten through 12th grade) or private university or college. (Pen. Code, § 626.9.)

Unauthorized Possession of a Firearm in a Courtroom, the State Capitol, etc.

It is illegal for any unauthorized person to bring or possess any firearm within a courtroom, courthouse, court building or at any meeting required to be open to the public. (Pen. Code, § 171b.)

It is illegal for any unauthorized person to bring or possess a loaded firearm within (including upon the grounds of) the State Capitol, any legislative office, any office of the Governor or other constitutional officer, any Senate or Assembly hearing room, the Governor's Mansion or any other residence of the Governor or the residence of any constitutional officer or any Member of the Legislature. For these purposes, a firearm shall be deemed loaded whenever both the firearm and its unexpended ammunition are in the immediate possession of the same person. (Pen. Code, §§ 171c, 171d, & 171e.)

Drawing or Exhibiting a Firearm

If another person is present, it is illegal for any person, except in self defense, to draw or exhibit a loaded or unloaded firearm in a rude, angry or threatening manner or in any manner use a firearm in a fight or quarrel. (Pen. Code, § 417.)

Threatening Acts with a Firearm on a Public Street or Highway

It is illegal for any person to draw or exhibit a loaded or unloaded firearm in a threatening manner against an occupant of a motor vehicle which is on a public street or highway in such a way that would cause a reasonable person apprehension or fear of bodily harm. (Pen. Code, § 417.3.)

Discharge of a Firearm in a Grossly Negligent Manner

It is illegal for any person to willfully discharge a firearm in a grossly negligent manner which could result in injury or death to a person. (Pen. Code, § 246.3.)

Discharge of a Firearm at an Inhabited/Occupied Dwelling, Building, Vehicle, Aircraft

It is illegal for any person to maliciously and willfully discharge a firearm at an inhabited dwelling, house, occupied building, occupied motor vehicle, occupied aircraft, inhabited house car or inhabited camper. (Pen. Code, § 246.)

Discharge of a Firearm at an Unoccupied Aircraft, Motor Vehicle, or Uninhabited Building or Dwelling

It is illegal for any person to willfully and maliciously discharge a firearm at an unoccupied aircraft. It is illegal for any person to discharge a firearm at an unoccupied motor vehicle, building or dwelling. This does not apply to an abandoned vehicle, an unoccupied motor vehicle or uninhabited building or dwelling with permission of the owner and if otherwise lawful. (Pen. Code, § 247.)

Discharge of a Firearm from a Motor Vehicle

It is illegal for any person to willfully and maliciously discharge a firearm from a motor vehicle. A driver or owner of a vehicle who allows any person to discharge a firearm from the vehicle may be punished by up to three years imprisonment in state prison. (Pen. Code, § 26100.)

Criminal Storage

"Criminal storage of firearm of the first degree" – Keeping any loaded firearm within any premises that are under your custody or control and you know or reasonably should know that a child (any person under 18) or a person prohibited from possessing a firearm or deadly weapon pursuant to state or federal law is likely to gain access to the firearm without the permission of the child's parent or legal guardian and the child or prohibited person obtains access to the firearm and thereby causes death or great bodily injury to himself, herself, or any other person. (Pen. Code, § 25100, subd. (a).)

"Criminal storage of firearm of the second degree" – Keeping any loaded firearm within any premises that are under your custody or control and you know or reasonably should know that a child (any person under 18) or a person prohibited from possessing a firearm or deadly weapon pursuant to state or federal law is likely to gain access to the firearm without the permission of the child's parent or legal guardian and the child or prohibited person obtains access to the firearm and thereby causes injury, other than great bodily injury, to himself, herself, or any other person, or carries the firearm either to a public place or in violation of Penal Code section 417. (Pen. Code, § 25100, subd. (b).)

"Criminal Storage of firearm of the third degree" – Keeping any loaded firearm within any premises that are under your custody or control and negligently storing or leaving a loaded firearm in a location where you know or reasonably should know that a child (any person under 18) is likely to gain access to the firearm without the permission of the child's parent or legal guardian, unless you have taken reasonable action to secure the firearm against access by the child. (Pen. Code, § 25100, subd. (c).)

None of the criminal storage offenses (first degree, second degree, third degree) shall apply whenever the firearm is kept in a locked container or locked with a locking device that has rendered the firearm inoperable. (Pen. Code, § 25105.)

Sales, Transfers and Loans of Firearms to Minors

Generally, it is illegal to sell, loan or transfer any long gun to a person under 18 years of age, or to sell a handgun to a person under 21 years of age. (Pen. Code, § 27505.)

Possession of a Handgun or Live Ammunition by Minors

It is unlawful for a minor to possess a handgun or live ammunition unless one of the following circumstances exists:

- The minor is accompanied by his or her parent or legal guardian and the minor is actively engaged in a lawful recreational sporting, ranching or hunting activity, or a motion picture, television or other entertainment event;

- The minor is accompanied by a responsible adult and has prior written consent of his or her parent or legal guardian and is involved in one of the activities cited above; or

- The minor is at least 16 years of age, has prior written consent of his or her parent or legal guardian, and the minor is involved in one of the activities cited above. (Pen. Code, §§ 29610-29655.)

PERSONS INELIGIBLE TO POSSESS FIREARMS

The following persons are prohibited from possessing firearms (Pen. Code, §§ 29800-29825, 29900; Welf. & Inst. Code, §§ 8100, 8103.):

Lifetime Prohibitions

- Any person convicted of any felony or any offense enumerated in Penal Code section 29905.

- Any person convicted of an offense enumerated in Penal Code section 23515.

- Any person with two or more convictions for violating Penal Code section

417, subdivision (a)(2).

- Any person adjudicated to be a mentally disordered sex offender. (Welf. & Inst. Code, § 8103, subd. (a)(1).)

- Any person found by a court to be mentally incompetent to stand trial or not guilty by reason of insanity of any crime, unless the court has made a finding of restoration of competence or sanity. (Welf. & Inst. Code, § 8103, subd. (b)(1), (c)(1), & (d)(1).)

10-Year Prohibitions

- Any person convicted of a misdemeanor violation of the following: Penal Code sections 71, 76, 136.5, 140, 148 (d), 171b, 171c, 171d, 186.28, 240, 241, 242, 243, 244.5, 245, 245.5, 246, 246.3, 247, 273.5, 273.6, 417, 417.1, 417.2, 417.6, 422, 626.9, 646.9, 830.95(a), 17500, 17510(a), 25300, 25800, 27510, 27590(c), 30315, or 32625, and Welfare and Institutions Code sections 871.5, 1001.5, 8100, 8101, or 8103.

5-Year Prohibitions

- Any person taken into custody as a danger to self or others, assessed, and admitted to a mental health facility under Welfare and Institutions Code sections 5150, 5151, 5152; or certified under Welfare and Institutions Code sections 5250, 5260, 5270.15.

Juvenile Prohibitions

- Juveniles adjudged wards of the juvenile court are prohibited until they reach age 30 if they committed an offense listed in Welfare and Institutions Code section 707, subdivision (b).

Miscellaneous Prohibitions

- Any person denied firearm possession as a condition of probation pursuant to Penal Code section 29900, subdivision (c).

- Any person charged with a felony offense, pending resolution of the matter. (18 U.S.C. § 922(g).)

- Any person while he or she is either a voluntary patient in a mental health facility or under a gravely disabled conservatorship (due to a mental disorder or impairment by chronic alcoholism) and if he or she is found to be a danger to self or others. (Welf. & Inst. Code, § 8103, subd. (e).)

- Any person addicted to the use of narcotics. (Pen. Code, § 29800, subd. (a).)

- Any person who communicates a threat (against any reasonably identifiable victim) to a licensed psychotherapist which is subsequently reported to law enforcement, is prohibited for five years. (Welf. & Inst. Code, § 8104, subd. (c).)

- Any person who is subject to a protective order as defined in Family Code section 6218, Penal Code section 136.2, or a temporary restraining order issued pursuant to Code of Civil Procedure sections 527.6 or 527.8.

1. It is illegal for a person convicted of any felony offense to possess a firearm. (page 43)

   True   False

2. To legally give a firearm to your best friend as a birthday gift, you must complete the transfer of the firearm through a licensed firearms dealer. (page 35)

   True   False

3. It is illegal to lend a firearm to a minor without the permission of the minor's parent or legal guardian. (page 43)

   True   False

4. Generally, a person may legally have a loaded firearm, if otherwise lawful, at his or her campsite. (page 39)

   True   False

5. It is illegal to buy, sell or possess a firearm knowing its identification marks have been erased or altered. (page 41)

   True   False

Answers: 1: True, 2: True, 3: True, 4: True, 5: True

Safe Handling Demonstration Glossary

Action: A series of moving parts that allow a firearm to be loaded, fired and unloaded.

Barrel: The metal tube through which a bullet passes on its way to a target.

Breech: The part of a firearm at the rear of the barrel.

Bullet: The projectile located at the tip of the cartridge case.

Caliber: The bullet or barrel diameter.

Cartridge: A single unit of ammunition made up of the case, primer, propellant and bullet.

Cartridge Case: A container for all other components which comprise a cartridge.

Chamber: The rear part of a gun barrel where the cartridge is located when the gun is loaded.

Cylinder: The part of a revolver that holds ammunition in individual chambers.

Cylinder Latch: A latch on double-action revolvers that allows the cylinder to swing out.

Double-Action: A type of firearm action in which a single pull of the trigger both cocks the hammer and releases it.

Dummy Round: A bright orange, red or other readily identifiable dummy round or an inert cartridge without powder and primer.

Ejector Rod: The part used to remove cartridges from the cylinder.

Grip: The handle of the firearm.

Hammer: The part of the firing mechanism which strikes the firing pin or primer.

Jam: A malfunction that prevents a firearm from firing properly.

Magazine: A separate box-like metal container for semi-automatic pistols into which cartridges are loaded.

Magazine Release: A device that releases the magazine so that it can be removed from the firearm.

Magazine Well: The opening in a firearm into which a magazine is inserted.

Muzzle: The front end of the barrel from which a bullet exits.

Revolver: A firearm that has a rotating cylinder containing a number of chambers.

Round: See cartridge.

Safety: A device on a firearm intended to help provide protection against accidental discharge under normal usage when properly engaged.

Semiautomatic pistol: A firearm that fires a single cartridge each time the trigger is pulled, and which automatically extracts and ejects the empty cartridge case and reloads the chamber.

Single-action: A type of firearm action in which pulling the trigger causes the hammer to release.

Trigger Guard: Located on the underside of the gun, the trigger guard is a rigid loop which particularly surrounds the trigger to prevent damage or accidental discharge.

If you have any comments or suggestions
regarding this publication, please send them to:

Department of Justice
Bureau of Firearms / FSC Unit
P.O. Box 160367
Sacramento, CA 95816-0367

or via our website at
http://oag.ca.gov/firearms

Printed on recycled paper